15 Easy-to-Read Biography Mini-Books: Famous Americans

by Susan Washburn Buckley

Thanks, Johnny Appleseed!

Helen Keller

Christopher Columbus Sets Sail

Pilgrim Children Helped Too!
Mary Allerton
Richard Moore

Squanto
The Pilgrims' Friend

A Special Learner

The Wright Brothers' First Flight

Martin Luther King, Jr.'s Dream

George Washington
Our First President

Abraham Lincoln
A Great President

Harriet Tubman
A Leader to F

Susan B. Anthony:
Fighter for Women's Rights

Roberto Clemente
A Star Player

Sally Ride's Great Ride

Dian Fossey
Friend to the Animals

Betsy Ross
Stars and Stripes

SCHOLASTIC
PROFESSIONAL BOOKS

New York • Toronto • London • Auckland • Sydney • Mexico City • New Delhi • Hong Kong

For Lorenzo,

who will soon be able to read these little books

Cover design by Norma Ortiz

Interior Design by Ellen Matlach Hassell
for Boultinghouse & Boultinghouse, Inc.

Cover and interior illustration by George Ulrich

ISBN 0-590-96718-5

Contents

Biography Mini-Books

Introduction

History is the story of the past, the story of people's lives. For all of us, but especially for children, exploring history as a story is far more engaging than learning history as facts. Each of these biography mini-books tells the story of an inspiring American who has made a difference—from Johnny Appleseed, a legendary traveler who planted apple seeds, to Sally Ride, a space traveler who flew on the *Challenger*. Each of these people can be seen as a role model in some way; each has characteristics or accomplishments that can inspire others to follow their own dreams.

While students are learning about these fascinating Americans, they'll also gain valuable reading practice. *15 Easy-to-Read Biography Mini-Books* provides a great way to integrate reading instruction into your social studies curriculum. The patterned, predictable text and appealing illustrations guide children as they begin to read independently. They'll love taking home these books to read again and again, to themselves and to others. Helping children develop "the reading habit" is one of the most valuable gifts that teachers can give.

The mini-books are organized by the months of the school year with suggested thematic links to events, anniversaries, or seasons. They can be easily integrated into the curriculum at other times of the year as well. Information and activities are provided on pages 5–17 to supplement each book. In this section, you'll find:

- Additional background information about each biography

- *Write About It!* a lively writing prompt on a topic related to the biography mini-book

- *Keep Going!* one or more activities to extend learning and tap into students' various learning styles

Have fun and happy reading!

Susan Washburn Buckley

How to Make the Mini-Books

1. Carefully remove the mini-book to be copied, tearing along the perforation.

2. Make a double-sided copy of the mini-book for each student. If your machine does not have a double-sided function, make copies of the title page first. (It is a good idea to make extra copies.) Then place these copies into the machine's paper tray. Next, make a test copy of the second page to make sure that it copies onto the back of the first page. It is important to check that the placement matches the original so that page 2 copies directly behind the title page.

3. Cut the page in half along the solid line.

4. Place page 3 behind the title page.

5. Fold the pages in half along the dotted line.

6. Check to be sure that the pages are in the proper order and then staple them together along the book's spine.

Background Information

September
Thanks, Johnny Appleseed!
1774–1845

September 26 is John Chapman's birthday and is celebrated today as Johnny Appleseed Day. John Chapman, known in history and legend as Johnny Appleseed, left home at the age of 20 and planted apple seeds across the new American frontier as far west as Indiana. According to legend, he wore a cooking pot on his head so that his hands would be free to hold a book he was reading. It is said that all of the apple trees that are now in the Midwest originated from Johnny Appleseed's trees.

The energy and determination of Johnny Appleseed can inspire children as they begin a new school year.

Write About It!
Give children this story starter. Suggest that they draw pictures to go with their stories.

If I could plant something all over the country, I would plant . . .

Keep Going!

- To show children how apples grow, cut an apple down the center. Ask children to point to the seeds. Explain that these are the kind of seeds that Johnny Appleseed planted. Tell children that it takes several years for an apple tree to grow and produce fruit. If possible, make applesauce as a class project to enjoy on Johnny Appleseed Day.

- Share with the class *The True Tale of Johnny Appleseed* by Margaret Hodges (Holiday House, 1997).

September
Helen Keller: A Special Learner
1880–1968

Helen Keller is a symbol of triumph over physical handicaps. When she was 19 months old, she became deaf and blind after she had a terrible fever. Eventually Helen's parents hired teacher Anne Sullivan to live with them and to work with Helen. A brilliant teacher, Anne taught six-year-old Helen to communicate. Sullivan used her fingers to spell out words on the palm of Helen's hand, guiding her to make the connection between words and objects. Understanding that "everything has a name" was the beginning of Helen Keller's remarkable ability to communicate in spite of the severe obstacles she faced. Helen Keller graduated from Radcliffe College in 1904. She wrote several books (which have been translated into more than 50 languages) and lectured around the world.

As the school year begins, the story of Helen Keller can help children understand that there are many ways to learn and that obstacles can be overcome with determination.

Write About It!
Ask children to write about a time when they had trouble learning something new. What did they do or what could they have done to help them succeed?

Keep Going!
- Have partners take turns spelling simple words with their fingers on each other's palms. Ask them to identify the words and discuss the challenges of communicating in this way.

- Place several objects in a bag without showing them to the class. Ask volunteers to reach into the bag and identify the objects using touch only. Discuss the challenges of identifying everything by touch, taste, or smell.

October
Christopher Columbus Sets Sail
1451(?)–1506

Although "the Admiral of the Ocean Sea" has become a controversial figure for several reasons, Christopher Columbus plays a key role in the story of our country. Columbus's treatment of the first Americans, the native people whom he encountered, cannot be ignored or justified. Nonetheless, his feats as a sailor and his determination as an explorer can be honored.

Columbus Day, celebrated on October 12, is a time to remember this great navigator and the other explorers who set in motion the European migration to the Americas. It is also a time to sensitize children to the effects of this migration on those who were already here and whose own societies were forever changed.

Write About It!
Tell children that Columbus's sailors urged him to turn back, doubting that they would ever find land. Columbus kept on, sure that he was right. Ask children to write a story called "Don't Give Up" about a time when they stuck to a dream or idea.

Keep Going!
- Help children trace Columbus's route from Spain to the Caribbean. (To simplify, use the area around the island of Grand Turk as his landing spot.)
- Tell the class that in Columbus's time, people believed that great sea monsters inhabited unknown oceans. Invite children to draw illustrations of imaginary sea monsters.

November

Pilgrim Children Helped Too!

Mary Allerton 1617–1699
Richard Moore 1614–1696

Of the 102 passengers who crossed the Atlantic on the *Mayflower* in 1620, 34 were children. Two others were born before the Pilgrims settled Plymouth. By the first Thanksgiving, there were 23 children in the community (and 29 adults). Having survived the perils of childhood in the seventeenth century, Mary Allerton and Richard Moore each lived to be over 80 years old!

Write About It!

Looking at the Thanksgiving story through the eyes of children who were there can make history come alive for students. Ask children to imagine that they were present at the first Thanksgiving. Have them write letters describing the day to family members or friends in England.

Keep Going!

- Discuss with the class the meaning of the word *thanksgiving* and talk about what the Pilgrims had to be thankful for. Ask children to write or draw pictures of what they are thankful for.

- Share with the class Kate Waters's books *Sarah Morton's Day* (Scholastic, 1989) and *Samuel Eaton's Day* (Scholastic, 1993), which tell the stories of Pilgrim children in words and photographs.

November

Squanto: The Pilgrims' Friend

?–1622

The Native American Squanto has become a symbol of friendship and survival. Both legend and scholarship claim that his aid was essential to the survival of the Plymouth community. Little is known of his life separate from the Pilgrims, but it is believed that he spent about ten years living in England after he was taken there in 1605. For the Pilgrims, it was a miracle that someone who spoke English came out of the woods to help them. Squanto showed the Pilgrims how to plant corn and where to fish, and he was their interpreter in communicating with Massasoit, the leader of the Native Americans of the region.

Learning about Squanto helps children remember that the story of Thanksgiving is broader than the experiences of the Pilgrims and deeper than the story of a meal.

Write About It!

Ask children to write a story about a time when they helped someone in an important way. How were they helpful?

Keep Going!

- Working in small groups, children can create mini-dramas about the first meeting between Squanto and the Pilgrims.
- Indian corn—similar to what Squanto planted with the Pilgrims—is often available during the Thanksgiving season. If possible, bring in ears of Indian corn and ordinary eating corn so that children can compare the two. The corn kernels can be used for sorting and can be glued onto paper to make patterns and designs.

December

The Wright Brothers' First Flight

Orville Wright 1871–1948

Wilbur Wright 1867–1912

A world without air flight is inconceivable to most of us. It is hard to believe that the first successful manned flight occurred less than 100 years ago and lasted for only 12 seconds! The Wright brothers' first successful flight took place on December 17, 1903, at Kitty Hawk, North Carolina. Wilbur and Orville Wright, bicycle makers by trade, tried to build a "flying machine" for seven years before their first real success. Based on weather advice, they went to the Atlantic beaches at Kitty Hawk for their flights. That first small airplane can be seen today in the National Air and Space Museum in Washington. It is the basis for every airplane flying today.

Write About It!

Ask children to write a description as if they were Orville Wright experiencing the world's first flight. How do they think he felt?

Keep Going!

Constructing paper airplanes can be an enjoyable learning experience. Fold paper into a paper airplane, sail it through the air, and ask children what made it fly. Help children understand that the shape of the wings enables the paper plane to stay in the air. Have children experiment with making and flying their own paper airplanes.

January
Martin Luther King, Jr.'s Dream
1929–1968

In a life that spanned less than 40 years, Martin Luther King, Jr. had a dramatic and lasting effect on American society. As a civil rights leader, he taught Americans the power of nonviolent protest against widespread racial inequality. In 1964 he was awarded the Nobel Peace Prize for his work. Just four years later, Dr. King was assassinated.

The story of Martin Luther King, Jr. is a catalyst for thinking about a number of profound issues: the inspiration that one person can provide, the power of nonviolent protest, and the injustice of discrimination. January 15 is a national holiday honoring the anniversary of Dr. King's birth.

Write About It!

Tell children about Dr. King's dream, expressed at the 1963 March on Washington, that our nation would one day act on the belief that all people are created equal. Ask them to write about their own dream for the United States.

Keep Going!

- Working in small groups, children can make posters commemorating Dr. Martin Luther King, Jr.

- Discuss with the class the ways that we can make our dreams come true. (Point out that we don't always succeed.) Have children make "dream books" in which they record and illustrate some of their goals and the ways they will accomplish them.

February
George Washington: Our First President

1732–1799

It was said that George Washington was "first in war, first in peace, and first in the hearts of his countrymen." As the general who led the new nation to victory in the Revolution, then as its first president, George Washington is an important symbol of the beginnings of the United States.

George Washington, whose birthday is February 22, is honored on Presidents' Day.

Write About It!

Ask children to imagine that they are going to be president of a brand new nation. Ask them to write a letter to a friend or family member explaining how they feel about their new role and their important responsibilities.

Keep Going!

- Remind children that our nation's capital was named for George Washington. Ask students: *If you could name a city after someone, who would it be and why?*

- Help children research other American presidents. Have each child choose one president to describe to the class.

February
Abraham Lincoln: A Great President

1809–1865

"Honest Abe," "the Railsplitter," "Father Abraham"—Abraham Lincoln is known as one of the greatest American Presidents. By steering the nation through the turmoil of the Civil War, he kept the United States "one nation, indivisible, with liberty and justice for all."

Abraham Lincoln was born on February 12 and is honored on Presidents' Day.

Write About It!

Ask children to imagine that they are president of the United States. Give them the writing prompt, *If I were president, I would . . .* and let them list or draw pictures of their most important goals.

Keep Going!

- Tell children that Abraham Lincoln was known for his honesty and was nicknamed "Honest Abe." Talk about what honesty is and why it is so important. Invite children to make posters about honesty.

- Discuss Abraham Lincoln's love of reading. Ask children to select a book that they love and tell the class about it.

February

Harriet Tubman: A Leader to Freedom

1820?–1913

Born into slavery, Harriet Tubman led so many fellow slaves to freedom that she was called "Moses." After her own escape from slavery in 1844, she helped more than 300 others flee via the Underground Railroad's network of aid. When the Civil War came, Tubman was a nurse and spy for the Union Army. Later she was active in the women's rights movement.

February is Black History Month. Harriet Tubman's escape to freedom and her courage in helping others are symbolic of the struggles and triumphs of African American history.

Write About It!

Discuss the concept of freedom with children. Ask students to write about what being free means to them.

Keep Going!

- Share with children Deborah Hopkinson's wonderful book about escape from slavery, *Sweet Clara and the Freedom Quilt* (Knopf, 1993).

- Design class posters for Black History Month honoring Harriet Tubman and others.

Susan B. Anthony:
Fighter for Women's Rights

March

Susan B. Anthony: Fighter for Women's Rights

1820–1906

Susan B. Anthony led the long and difficult fight to gain rights for women in this country. It was not until 1920, after Anthony's death, that American women gained the right to vote with the passage of the 19th Amendment to the Constitution. Anthony began her activist career in the temperance movement, working to abolish the consumption of alcoholic beverages. By the 1850s she had joined forces with Elizabeth Cady Stanton. The two embarked on a vigorous and ultimately successful campaign to gain equal rights for women.

March is National Women's History Month. Susan B. Anthony stands as a symbol of women's strength as well as their struggle to gain equal rights.

Write About It!

After discussing why, when, and how citizens vote in the United States, have children write letters to the local newspaper urging adults to vote in the next election. Ask children to list the reasons voting is important.

Keep Going!

- Show the class a Susan B. Anthony dollar, explaining that Anthony was the first woman pictured on an American coin. Children can work in small groups to select other women they would like to honor with a coin. Invite groups to design their proposed coins and display them for the class.

- Present to the class information about the next local, state, or national election. Have a mock vote in class.

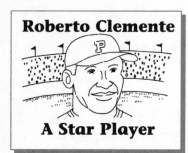

April

Roberto Clemente:
A Star Player

1934–1972

An outstanding baseball player, Roberto Clemente became a national hero after he died en route to help Nicaraguan earthquake victims. Clemente was born in Puerto Rico and moved from the island baseball leagues to mainland teams. He played for the Pittsburgh Pirates from 1955 until his death. Clemente was a highly honored player who used his celebrity to support worthy causes.

The opening of baseball season in the spring is a good time for students to think about attributes they admire in sports figures, from strength and speed to sportsmanship.

Write About It!

Give children this story starter: *My favorite person in sports is . . .* Ask them to describe the person and explain why he or she is their favorite.

Keep Going!

- Roberto Clemente was twice chosen Most Valuable Player. Ask each child to choose a Most Valuable "Player" in his or her own life.

- Discuss with the class Clemente's belief that it is important to help people who are in danger or have less than you do. Help the class choose a project or cause that they would like to support. Investigate ways children's efforts can make a difference.

Dian Fossey

Friend to the Animals

May

Dian Fossey: Friend to the Animals

1932–1985

Be Kind to Animals Week takes place during the first week of May. The story of Dian Fossey is a perfect example of kindness to animals. Dian Fossey spent nearly 20 years isolated in the Virunga Volcanoes in Rwanda so that she could observe the majestic mountain gorilla. Before her study, little was known about these creatures, whose existence was seriously threatened. Fossey was outraged by the cruelty that hunters inflicted upon gorillas, who were often caught in traps set for other animals or killed so that their feet and heads could be sold as souvenirs. Although Fossey helped educate the public about the plight of the mountain gorilla, she also angered people who did not agree with her views. In 1985, Dian was killed in her cabin at the research site. She inspired others to take up her worthy cause, and work continues today on learning about and protecting gorillas.

Write About It!

Have students imagine they are Dian Fossey writing in her journal after her first day in the wilderness. How does it feel to be alone in a new place?

Keep Going!

- Invite a volunteer from a local ASPCA to discuss ways children can care for animals. Have students make posters about what they learned.

- Ask students to observe an animal, such as a goldfish, bird, cat, dog, or even an ant. Then have them share with the class what they have learned about this creature's habits.

May

Sally Ride's Great Ride

1959–

In June 1983, Sally Kristen Ride became the first American woman to travel in space. Trained as a physicist, Dr. Ride entered the astronaut program in 1978. During her first six-day flight on the space shuttle *Challenger*, she launched communications satellites, conducted pharmaceutical experiments, and tested the shuttle's remote control arm. She made a second shuttle flight in 1984. After the *Challenger* exploded in 1986, Sally Ride was part of the commission that investigated the tragedy. She left the space program in 1987 and became a professor of physics and director of a space institute.

May is an appropriate time to honor Americans who "take to the air." Sally Ride's birthday is May 26. On May 5, 1961, Alan Shepard was the first American to travel in space. And on May 15, 1927, Charles Lindbergh made his record-breaking transatlantic flight.

Write About It!

Ask children if they would like to travel into outer space. Where in the universe would they most like to go? To the moon? To Mars? Have them write about and draw pictures of an imagined trip on a space shuttle.

Keep Going!

- Invite children to draw pictures of what Sally Ride might have seen when she was flying on the space shuttle.

- Show children photographs from books of how the astronauts live on a space shuttle. Ask students to imagine what it would be like to do everyday things like eating and sleeping in a place where there is no gravity.

June

Betsy Ross: Stars and Stripes

1752–1836

The story of Betsy Ross making the first American flag may be true or it may be legend. Historians are not sure. It is known, however, that Betsy Ross was a seamstress in Philadelphia during the American Revolution. And it is known that she made flags. In 1870 Betsy Ross's grandson reported that his grandmother had told him the story of how she made the first official flag for the United States at the request of General George Washington.

The flag that Betsy Ross is said to have made became the nation's official flag on June 14, 1777. This date is celebrated every year as Flag Day.

Write About It!

Ask children to imagine that they are Betsy Ross on the day General Washington came to ask for the flag. Have them write a journal entry describing their feelings about this important task.

Keep Going!

- Show students their state flag and lead a discussion about the meaning of its symbols.
- Have children work in small groups to design flags for your class or school.

4

John planted apple seeds all over the United States.

They grew into beautiful apple trees.

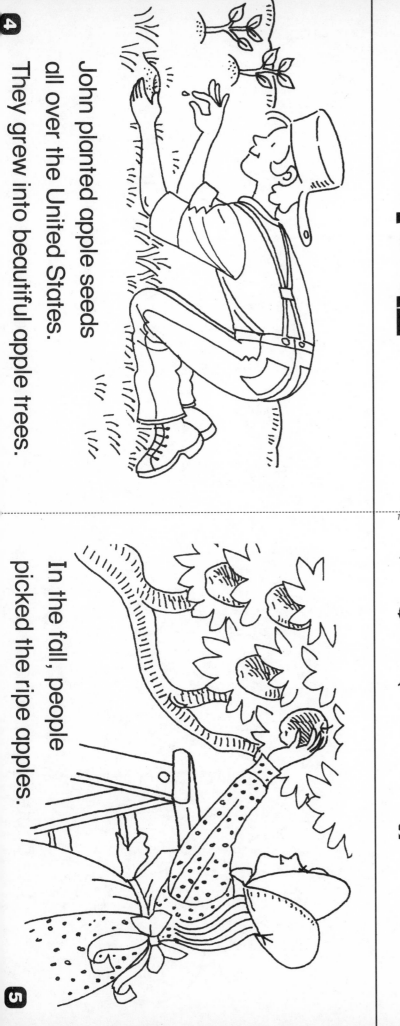

Thanks, Johnny Appleseed!

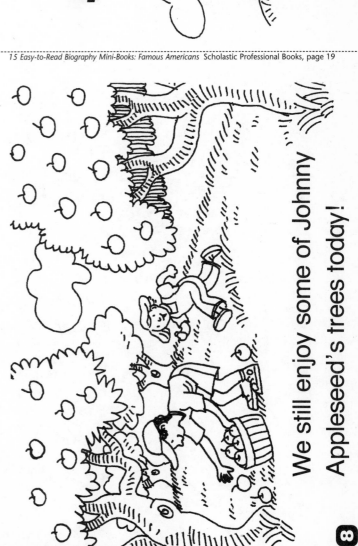

5

In the fall, people picked the ripe apples.

8

We still enjoy some of Johnny Appleseed's trees today!

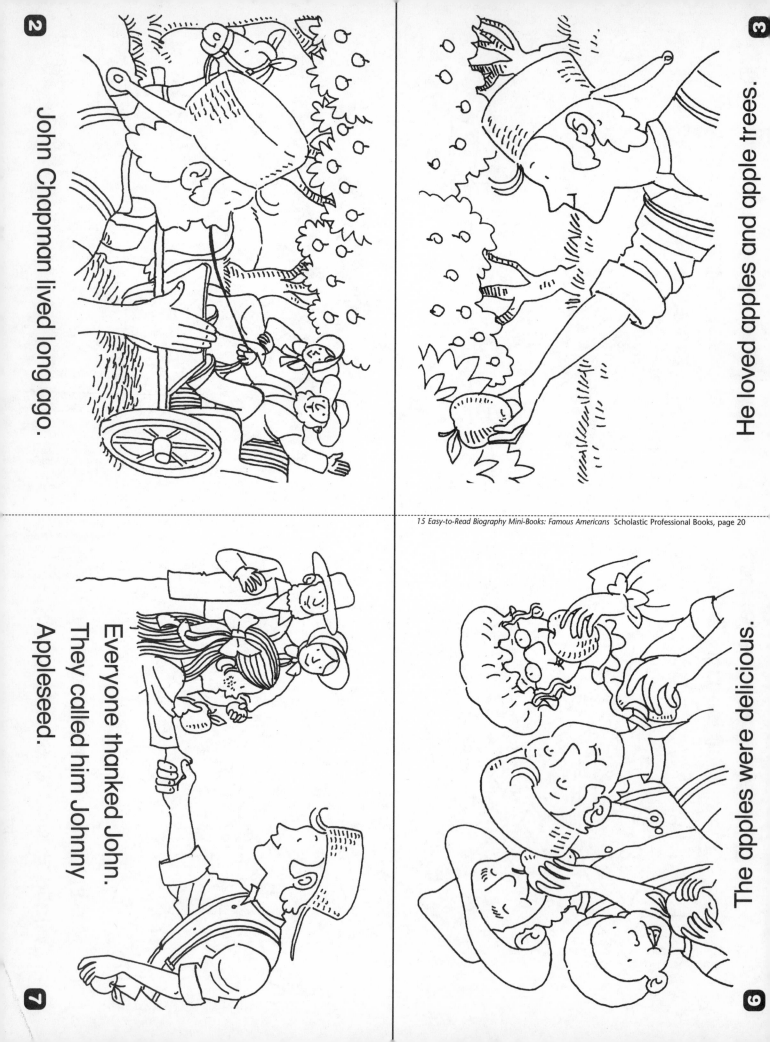

2

John Chapman lived long ago.

3

He loved apples and apple trees.

7

Everyone thanked John.
They called him Johnny
Appleseed.

6

The apples were delicious.

4

Helen had her own teacher named Anne Sullivan.

Helen Keller

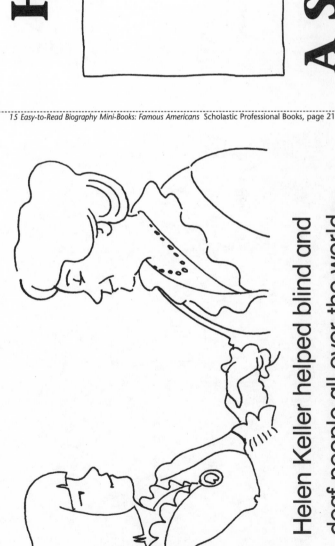

A Special Learner

5

Anne spelled words on Helen's hands. Helen learned that there are words for everything.

8

Helen Keller helped blind and deaf people all over the world.

2

Helen Keller could not see or hear anything.

3

She learned in special ways.

7

When Helen grew older, she gave speeches and wrote books.

6

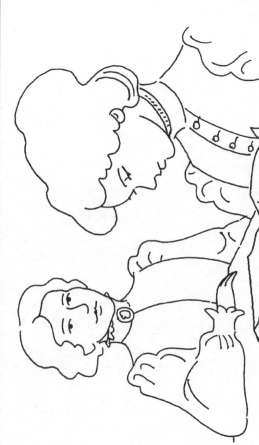

Anne helped Helen learn to read and write.

4

In 1492, Columbus sailed from Spain. He wanted to find riches in China and India.

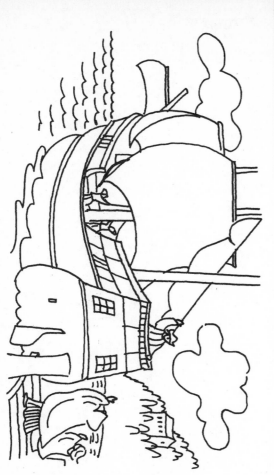

Christopher Columbus Sets Sail

5

He had 90 brave sailors and 3 small ships: the *Nina*, the *Pinta*, and the *Santa Maria*.

8

We remember Columbus every year on October 12.

3

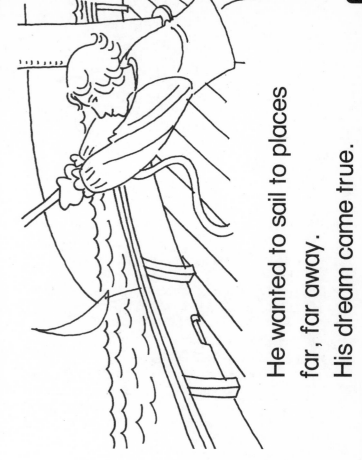

He wanted to sail to places
far, far away.
His dream came true.

2

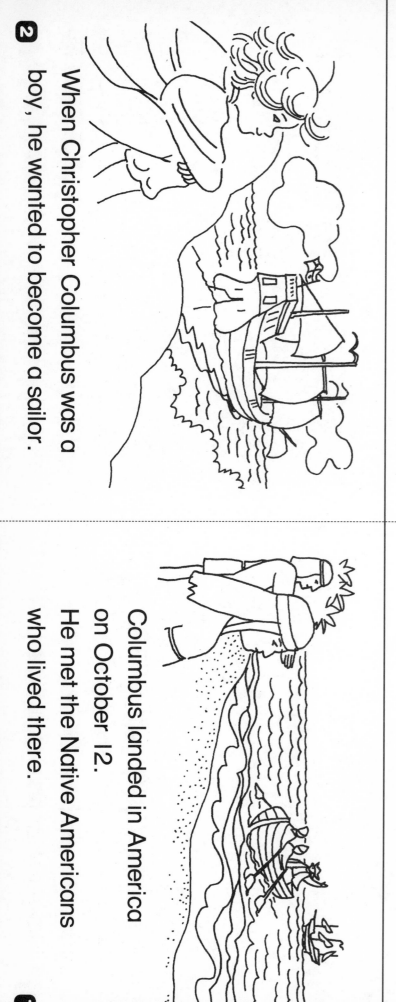

When Christopher Columbus was a
boy, he wanted to become a sailor.

6

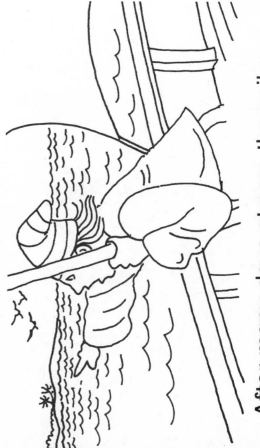

After many days at sea, the sailors
saw land!
But it was neither China nor India.

7

Columbus landed in America
on October 12.
He met the Native Americans
who lived there.

Pilgrim Children Helped Too!

Richard Moore

Mary Allerton

A

The Pilgrims gathered nuts and berries.
Mary and Richard helped.

5

The Pilgrims farmed the land.
Mary and Richard helped.

8

The Pilgrims gave thanks
for their new home.
Mary and Richard gave thanks too.

In America, the Pilgrims built homes.
Mary and Richard helped.

15 Easy-to-Read Biography Mini-Books: Famous Americans Scholastic Professional Books, page 26

The Pilgrims prepared a feast.
Mary and Richard helped.

In 1620, Mary and Richard sailed
to America on the *Mayflower*.

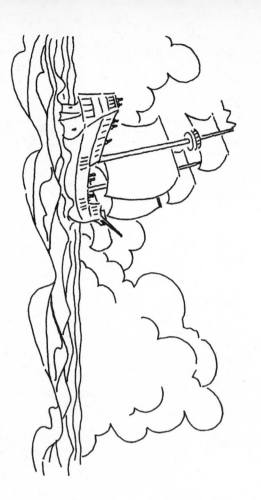

The Pilgrims shared the feast with
their Native American neighbors.
Mary and Richard shared too.

4

He helped the Pilgrims find places to fish.

5

He helped the Pilgrims find herbs and berries.

Squanto

The Pilgrims' Friend

15 Easy-to-Read Biography Mini-Books: Famous Americans Scholastic Professional Books, page 27

The Pilgrims were thankful that Squanto was their friend.

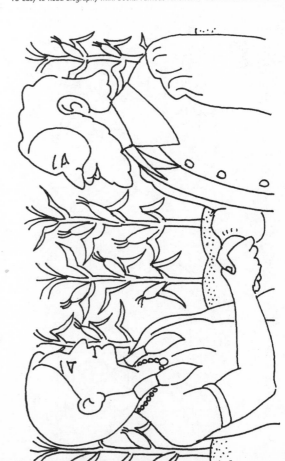

8

2

Squanto was a Native American.
He became the Pilgrims' good friend.

3

Squanto helped the Pilgrims grow corn.

7

He helped the Pilgrims celebrate the first Thanksgiving.

6

He helped the Pilgrims meet other Native Americans.

When they were older, they wanted to build a flying machine.

The Wright Brothers' First Flight

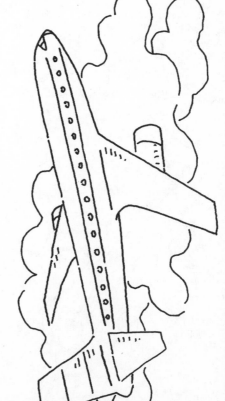

They watched birds to learn how they fly.

The Wright brothers taught other people how to build planes. They helped change our world forever.

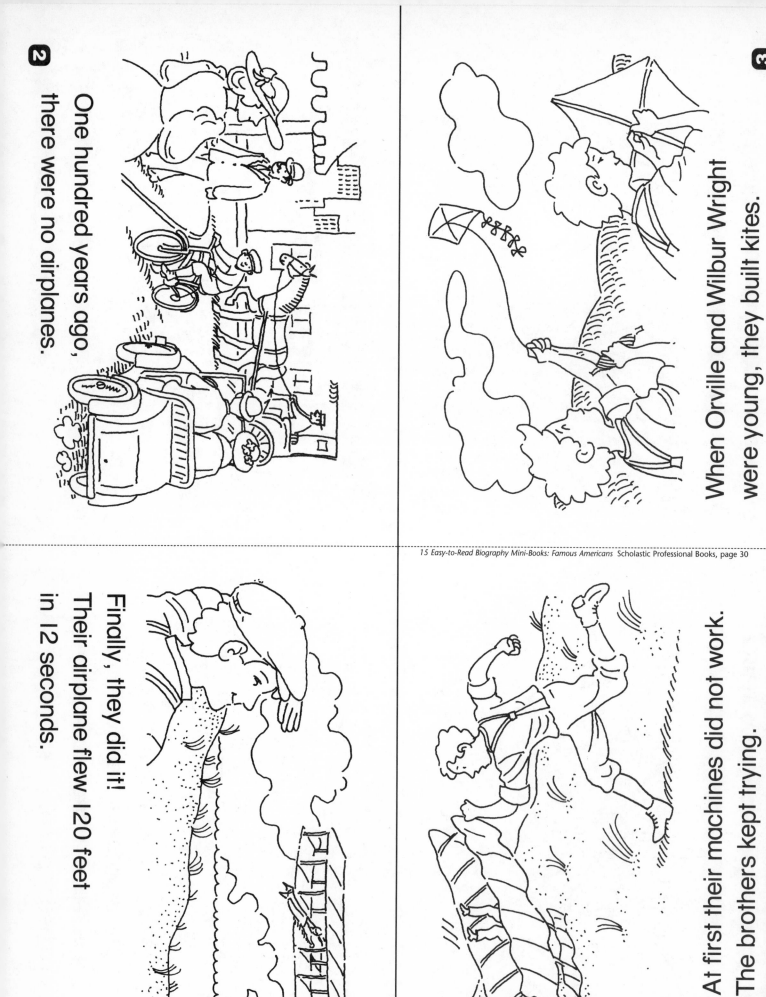

2

One hundred years ago, there were no airplanes.

3

When Orville and Wilbur Wright were young, they built kites.

7

Finally, they did it! Their airplane flew 120 feet in 12 seconds.

6

At first their machines did not work. The brothers kept trying.

4

Martin Luther King, Jr. worked to make his dream come true.

Martin Luther King, Jr.'s Dream

He wrote about his dream.

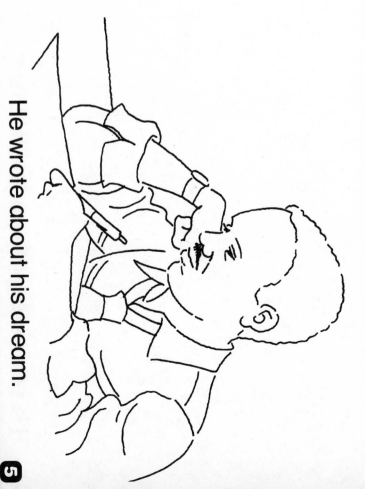

5

Martin Luther King, Jr. was a great leader.
He helped make our country a better place.

8

3

In his dream, all people were equal.

6

He gave speeches about his dream.

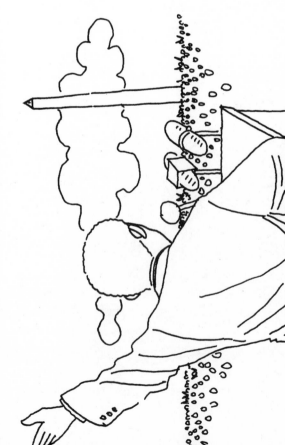

2

Martin Luther King, Jr. had a dream.

7

He wanted people everywhere to share his dream of equality.

His bravery helped our country win its freedom.

George Washington

Our First President

15 Easy-to-Read Biography Mini-Books: Famous Americans Scholastic Professional Books, page 33

George Washington was the first president of the new nation, the United States.

We honor George Washington on Presidents' Day.

When George Washington was a boy,
England ruled America.

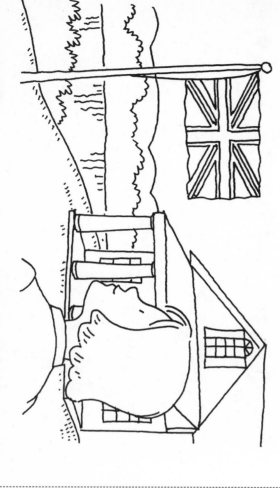

When he grew up, he was a general
in the Revolutionary War.

Our nation's capital was named
for George Washington.

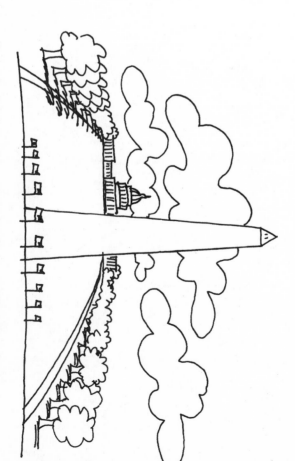

As president, he worked to
make the new nation strong.

4

People liked him everywhere he went.
They called him "Honest Abe."

Abraham Lincoln

A Great President

5

Abraham Lincoln was elected president of the United States.

We honor Abraham Lincoln on Presidents' Day.

8

2

Abraham Lincoln grew up in a log cabin.
He farmed the land with his father.

3

Young Abe loved to read and learn.

7

He helped pass a law that ended slavery.

6

Abraham Lincoln led the nation in the Civil War.

4

Then Harriet helped hundreds of slaves run away too.

5

She showed them where to hide.

Harriet Tubman

A Leader to Freedom

8

Today all Americans are free.

Brave Harriet ran away to freedom.

Harriet Tubman grew up in slavery.

She showed them how to follow the North Star to freedom.

Harriet Tubman was a brave woman. She wanted all people to be free.

4

She talked to people everywhere.

Susan B. Anthony:
Fighter for Women's Rights

5

She marched in parades and carried signs.

Susan B. Anthony is a hero.
She helped all American women.

8

3

Susan B. Anthony worked
to change the laws.

2

Long ago, laws said only men could vote.
Women could not vote.

VOTE

GIVE THE VOTE TO WOMEN

6

She wrote letters and books
about women's rights.

7

In 1920, the laws were changed.
Women won the right to vote.

A

He had 3,000 hits altogether!

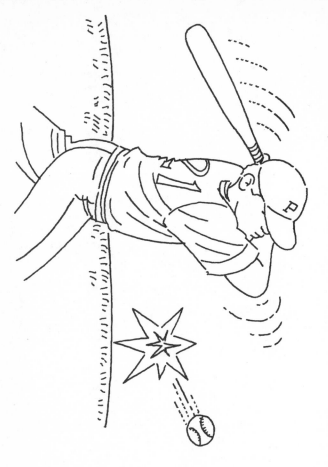

Roberto Clemente

A Star Player

5

Roberto had many fans.
He liked to meet them.

8

Roberto was named
"Most Valuable Player."
Two years later, he was elected
to the Baseball Hall of Fame.

MOST VALUABLE PLAYER

PIRATES

2

Roberto Clemente grew up in Puerto Rico.
He loved to play baseball.

3

He played baseball with the Pittsburgh Pirates for 17 years.

7

In 1971, Roberto's team won the World Series.

6

Roberto helped children play sports in Puerto Rico.
He built a place for them to play.

She learned what they eat.
She learned how they play.

2

Dian Fossey

Friend to the Animals

She learned how they
take care of their babies.

5

Dian Fossey believed that
animals are our friends.

8

2

Dian Fossey loved animals. She went to Africa to study mountain gorillas.

3

Dian spent many years watching the gorillas.

7

Dian also worked hard to protect the gorillas from hunters.

NO HUNTING

6

Then Dian wrote a book to share what she learned about gorillas.

One of the astronauts was Sally Ride.
She was the first American woman
in space.

Sally Ride's Great Ride

5

Sally worked hard on the shuttle.
She helped Americans learn
about space.

Space Facts

February 20, 1962
First American in space

July 16, 1969
Americans land on the moon

April 12, 1981
First space shuttle flies around Earth

2

10 9 8 7 6 5 4 3 2 1 . . .

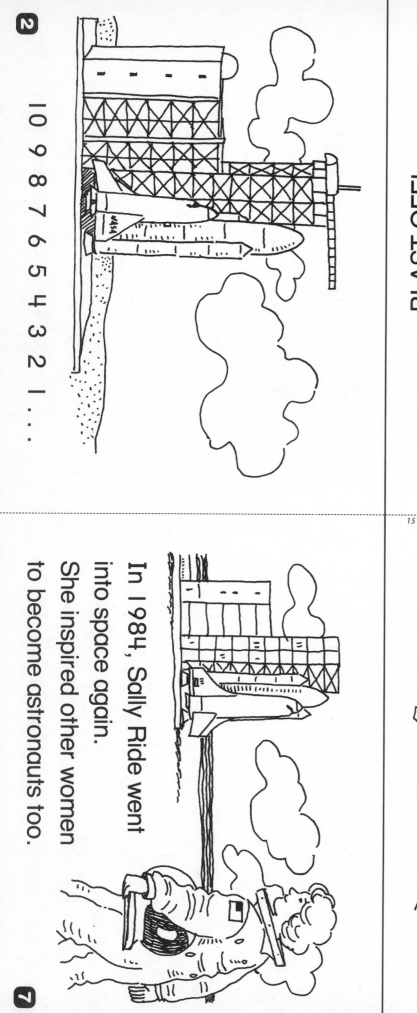

. . . BLAST OFF!

In June 1983, the space shuttle *Challenger* blasted into space.

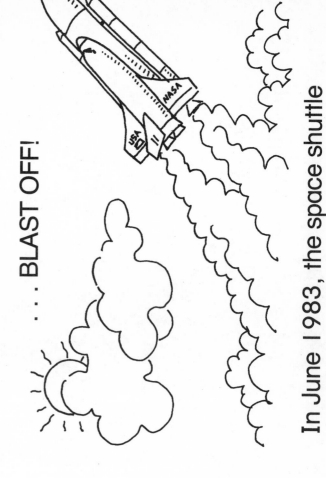

6

After six days, the astronauts came home.

7

In 1984, Sally Ride went into space again. She inspired other women to become astronauts too.

There were 13 states in
the new nation.
They say Betsy Ross made
one star for each state.

A

Betsy Ross

Stars and Stripes

15 Easy-to-Read Biography Mini-Books: Famous Americans Scholastic Professional Books, page 47

They say Betsy Ross made
one stripe for each state.

5

June 14 is Flag Day.
We remember the story of Betsy
Ross and her flag.

8

2

Long ago, our country fought a war to be free. America needed a flag.

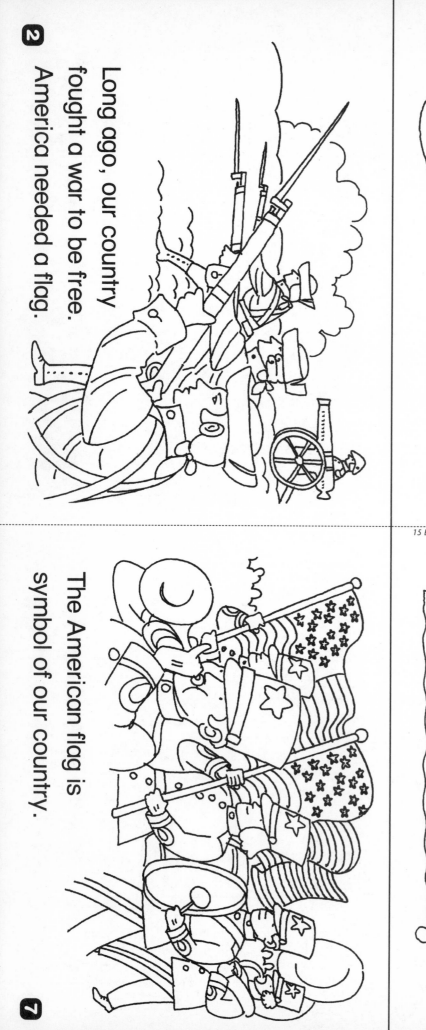

3

Some people say that George Washington asked Betsy Ross to make the first flag.

7

The American flag is symbol of our country.

6

Today there are 50 states. Today our flag has 50 stars and 13 stripes.

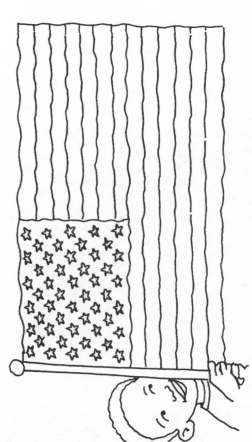